Find Frosty

as He Sings Christmas Carols

Illustrated by Jerry Tiritilli

Manufactured in the U.S.A.

8 7 6 5 4 3 2

ISBN 1-56173-162-5

Frosty the Snowman
Copyright © 1950 by Hill & Range Songs, Inc. Copyright renewed, controlled by Chappel & Co. Inc., (Intersong Music, Publisher).

Santa Claus Is Comin' to Town
Copyright © 1934 (renewed 1961) Leo Feist, Inc.

Rudolph the Red-Nosed Reindeer
Copyright © 1949 St. Nicholas Music Inc., renewed 1977.

All I Want for Christmas Is My Two Front Teeth
Copyright © 1947 M. Witmark & Sons. Renewed 1974.

Deck the Halls
Copyright © 1930, G. Schirmer, Inc.

Up on the Housetop
Copyright © 1931, Lillie Ellis Ferguson.

O Christmas Tree
Copyright © 1933, Mid-Town Music Company.

PUBLICATIONS INTERNATIONAL, LTD.

Frosty, the snowman
Was a jolly, happy soul!

Hey! This song is about *me!* I made a lot of friends that day the children put a magic top hat on my head and a broomstick in my hand! Boy, were they surprised when I began to sing and dance around! Can you find me? Can you find my friends who chased me here and there, all around the square, playing catch-me-if-you-can?

Kevin

Mark

Lee

Chris

Michael

Claire

Scotty

Jenny

Deck the halls with boughs of holly,
  Fa la la la la la la la la!
'Tis the season to be jolly,
  Fa la la la la la la la la!

There's no time like Christmastime for putting up lots of decorations! These folks are really getting into the spirit of the season. Can you find these decorations? Do you see me?

A snowman ornament

Boughs of holly

A candy cane

A drum ornament

The treetop angel

A jingle-bell wreath

An angel centerpiece

A snowman snow dome

Rudolph, the red-nosed reindeer
Had a very shiny nose . . . !

Rudolph was different from the other
reindeer—his nose glowed! The other
reindeer thought Rudolph was strange.
They didn't ask him to join in their
games. One Christmas Eve, Santa
made Rudolph a hero. Can you find
the nine reindeer who pulled Santa's
sleigh that foggy night? Do you see
me, too?

Dasher   Dancer   Prancer

Vixen   Comet   Cupid

Donder   Blitzen   Rudolph

CHRISTMAS IS:

DECEMBER

All I want for
Chrithmath ith my
Two front teeth!

My friend the Tooth Fairy must be flat
broke! The kids in this crazy classroom
are losing their teeth left and right!
How do you suppose they "thing"
Christmas carols? See if you can spot
these kids who are missing their front
teeth. Can you find me, too?

Scott

Silvester

Sally

Sandy

Simon

Suzannah

Sean

Sydney

Silver bells, silver bells,
  It's Christmastime in the city . . . .

This big city is full of the sounds of Christmas. People are laughing, taxis are honking their horns, and above all the noise is the sound of silver bells. After you have found me, look for these "treasures" that shoppers are taking home.

A television

A dolly

A globe

A red bicycle

A robot

A panda bear

This wrapped gift

A puppy

A piano

U p on the house-top
Reindeer pause . . . .

Ho, ho, ho! Old St. Nick has always brought special toys for little Nell and little Bill. He's checking to see if they have taken good care of their toys. Do you see him? Can you find . . .

A dolly that laughs and cries

A hammer

A ball

A train

A jump rope

A rubber duckie

A bicycle

A guitar

. . . and me, Frosty?

O Christmas tree,
O Christmas tree,
How lovely are your branches!

Now here's a little town that means business when it is time to decorate Christmas trees!

Can you find my favorite ornaments? I'll give you a hint: The trees each match a store. After you've admired the decorations, see if you can find me!

Dog bone

Pink ornament

High-heeled shoe

Slice of pie

Wrench

Lollipop

Button

Panda bear

Music note

Santa Claus is comin' To town!

Santa Claus always checks his list twice to be sure he hasn't made a mistake. He also keeps track of who is naughty and who is nice all year. (I'll tell you a little secret: He puts a check by your name if you cry or pout too often!) Can you find four naughty kids and four nice kids? Can you find me, too?

Naughty

Nice

Naughty

Nice

Naughty

Nice

Naughty

Nice

J

Jingle bells,
Jingle bells,
Jingle all the way!
Oh, what fun it is to ride
In a one-horse open sleigh!

Everyone seems to be enjoying a sleigh ride today! The air is filled with the jingle of harness bells. There are lots of other bells in this picture, too. Can you find them? Do you also see me hiding?

A green strap of jingle bells

A cow bell

A southern belle

A bell choir

A church bell

A bellhop

A belly flop

Take another look at *Jingle Bells.*
Can you find eight more "bells"?

- ☐ Bell bottoms
- ☐ Bluebells
- ☐ Bell pepper
- ☐ Dumbbell
- ☐ Belly laugh
- ☐ Belly dancer
- ☐ Bellyache
- ☐ Barbell

Go back to *Frosty, the Snowman* and see if you can find these funny things.

- ☐ A dog dressed like its master
- ☐ Two snow officers
- ☐ A singing jailbird
- ☐ A huntsman who's found a "fox"
- ☐ An invisible pet
- ☐ A crazy eight ball
- ☐ "Saw"-berry shortcake
- ☐ A leaky customer

Lots of things went wrong in *Deck the Halls!* Can you find these disasters?

- ☐ A wobbling ladder
- ☐ Two people slipping
- ☐ A toddler toppling a poinsettia
- ☐ A runaway sled
- ☐ Faulty wiring
- ☐ A guest who forgot her dress
- ☐ A tinsel fight
- ☐ A pie in the face

Can you find these reindeer games in *Rudolph, the Red-Nosed Reindeer?*

- ☐ Marbles
- ☐ Checkers
- ☐ Pin-the-tail-on-the-reindeer
- ☐ Jump-rope
- ☐ Baseball
- ☐ Hopscotch
- ☐ Cards
- ☐ Video

Can you find these eight classroom disasters in *All I Want for Christmas is my Two Front Teeth?*

- ☐ "Finger painting"
- ☐ A bad science experiment
- ☐ A frog down a collar
- ☐ A bowl of soup on a head
- ☐ A worm in an apple
- ☐ A kid stuck to his chair
- ☐ A bookworm
- ☐ Ants in some pants